The Student in Higher Education

REPORT OF THE COMMITTEE ON THE STUDENT

IN HIGHER EDUCATION

The Committee on the Student in Higher Education

Members:

Joseph F. Kauffman, *Chairman*
Dean of Student Affairs, University of Wisconsin

Grace Ann Carroll
Former Student Leader, Barat College of the Sacred Heart

Alan Frank, M. D.
Psychiatrist, Ritenour Health Center, Pennsylvania State University

Donald H. Ford
Dean, College of Human Development, Pennsylvania State University

Andrew M. Greeley
Senior Study Director, National Opinion Research Center, University of Chicago

Garlan E. Hoskin
Administrative Assistant, The Hazen Foundation

Joseph Katz
Associate Director, Institute for the Study of Human Problems, Stanford University

Kenneth Keniston
Associate Professor of Psychology, Yale University School of Medicine

Esther Raushenbush
President, Sarah Lawrence College

Philip Sherburne
Student, Harvard University Law School, formerly President of the United States National Student Association

Committee on the Student in Higher Education

The Student in Higher Education

January 1968

Additional copies of this book may be obtained from:

The Hazen Foundation
New Haven, Connecticut 06511

Library of Congress Catalog Card Number: 68-19177

Printed in U.S.A.

Contents

Foreword

THE COMMITTEE ON the Student in Higher Education was appointed by the Hazen Foundation early in 1966, with Joseph F. Kauffman, dean of student affairs at the University of Wisconsin, as chairman. The Committee's primary concern has been to gain perspective on the various social and psychological influences which shape student attitudes, interests, and activities. This has been a particularly auspicious time to carry on these deliberations because of the many manifestations of awakened student interests and concerns throughout the country.

This essay is the result of the work of the Committee over a period of some 18 months. It is addressed to administrators, students, teachers, and others who share a desire to improve the college experience, both for students and the larger society.

This report, then, is not a research study or an empirical survey, but a statement of a position. We have among us a great deal of varied experience. We have read, talked, reflected, and argued. What follows is a statement of the position which evolved from our discussions. Each of us might have wanted to stress some ideas more than others or express them a little differently. But despite these differences in emphasis and style, our report reflects an agreement on certain basic issues. We hope that this statement will cause others to think and especially to act.

The Committee owes a debt of gratitude to Andrew M. Greeley who prepared the final draft of this report. We are also indebted to Theodore J. Marchese who helped prepare preliminary drafts, and to Mrs. Rhoda Pauley who edited the manuscript for publication. We are grateful to the trustees of the Hazen Foundation who initiated this inquiry, appointed the Committee, supported its efforts in financial and other ways, and have now issued the report on our behalf.

Joseph F. Kauffman, *Chairman*
Grace Ann Carroll
Alan Frank, M. D.
Donald H. Ford
Andrew M. Greeley

Garlan E. Hoskin
Joseph Katz
Kenneth Keniston
Esther Raushenbush
Philip Sherburne

I

Introduction

THE AMERICAN UNIVERSITY is one of the most impressive social institutions devised by modern man. It has demonstrated a remarkable ability to maintain a continuity with its own past and at the same time keep up with our society's rapidly changing needs. Scarcely more than a generation ago, its major instructional concerns were to provide preprofessional training for the technical elites needed to keep our society operating and a gentleman's liberal education for the offspring of the well-to-do. Its research was of secondary importance, produced by a creative minority of faculty members, usually working as isolated scholars at a pace rarely exceeding the leisurely.

But since the end of the second world war, U.S. colleges and universities have assumed responsibility for offering post-high school education to almost everyone who desires it—regardless, in many instances, of why they desire it. At present almost half of our high school graduates are or have been enrolled at a college or university and the goal of college for Everyman is rarely exposed to serious challenge. During the same two-decade period, university research has grown into an immense and vital industry, providing the theoretical bases and the technical skills needed to keep our highly dynamic society functioning and growing.

It is very easy to criticize the failures of American higher education; indeed anyone who gives more than a quarter hour of serious thought to the subject can find much to criticize in any educational

3

effort man has ever undertaken. The Committee which is presenting this report to the American public finds much to criticize in American higher education, but the Committee members also share a deep respect for the accomplishments of the university, which has expanded its facilities and services at a phenomenal rate, particularly during the past quarter century, not only without deterioration of the quality of classroom instruction, but even more impressive, with considerable improvement in this quality.

However, dissatisfaction with past accomplishments is an ancient American tradition. Just as the political leader is asked by his constituency, "What have you done for us lately?" and the employer is confronted by the demand of his workers for "More!," so higher education must be required to shoulder a new burden, though one which represents an expansion of a responsibility that has long been perceived. The Committee proposes to criticize American higher education for not being more concerned about the total personality development of its students.

We are not harkening back to a mythical golden age when the college did indeed educate the "whole man"; but we are rather asking that the college do more than it ever did before in facilitating the development of the young adult personality. We are not arguing that men of good will and intelligence have failed to actively seek this goal, but we are saying that they find themselves impeded by organizational structures that prevent both faculty and administration from engaging in the kinds of educational innovation which are necessary to achieve such goals.

This criticism does not mean that the American university has failed, but rather that its very successes impose upon it a whole set of new obligations, particularly to do more than ever before to educate "the whole man." Men of good will and intelligence have always sought this end, and there are educators today still seeking it. But they find themselves blocked by more obstacles than ever before because the university has changed so much. Its sprawling size and organizational structure stand in the way of the innovations needed to reach this end.

The goals recommended in this report are not a response to student radicalism. On the contrary, the lack of educational radicalism among student reformers is rather disappointing. Their demands generally focus on the political and social life of the institution but, with rare

4

exception, show little concern for improving the quality of the educational enterprise itself. In fact many faculty members and administrators seem more upset with the slow progress of college instruction than student radicals are.

The Committee is therefore quite aware that in asking the college to assume more conscious responsibility for the human development of its students, it is asking for something that has never been done before, despite frequent promises in catalogues. We make our demands for two related reasons: 1) Our increased sophistication in the behavioral sciences gives us enough understanding of the process of human development to make the integration of the cognitive growth of the human personality with the noncognitive technically possible. Much remains to be discovered about personality development of the young adult, but much is also known. Our educational procedures rarely take cognizance of what we do know about human development. 2) We sense further that the national conscience is vaguely aware that something more is possible in higher education and must be done. Restlessness, apathy, alienation, and drug abuse have prodded the national conscience into the realization that something is missing in higher education, and its absence was much less noticeable in the days before affluence and mass higher education. We therefore hope, perhaps with inexcusable presumption, that the major impact of this report will be to contribute to the clarification of the national conscience.

Educating the "Whole Man"

Our basic assumption is that the college is a major agent in promoting the personality development of the young adult. Whether it realizes it or not, the college has a major effect upon the development of the whole human personality for the student between the ages of 17 and 25. Moreover, the young person becomes what he becomes not *only* because of what he hears in the classroom and not even *mainly* because of what he hears in the classroom. His interaction with teachers, his encounter with the social structure of the college administration, the friendship groups in which he becomes integrated, the values he acquires from student culture, the atmosphere of flexibility or rigidity which permeates the school environment, the playfulness or the seriousness, the "practicality" or the "spontaneity" of

5

operative educational goals of his college—all these have an immense, if not yet precisely measured, impact on the evolution of the young person's self view and world view, on his confidence and altruism, on his mastering of the needs for identity and intimacy. The college cannot escape the fact that it does have such an impact, that the quality of life on the campus (and even in the halls of the commuter college) does shape the personality of its youthful charges. By the very fact that it presumes to inform the minds of the young, the college becomes involved in the development of the whole person, of which the intellectual faculties are but a part. The time has come for the college to realize the extent of its power to influence personality development and to take full responsibility for the way this power is executed.

Despite our limited behavioral knowledge, the college must recognize that even its instructional goals cannot be effectively achieved unless it assumes some responsibility for facilitating the development of the total human personality. A student is not a passive digester of knowledge elegantly arranged for him by superior artists of curriculum design. He listens, reads, thinks, studies, and writes at the same time that he feels, worries, hopes, loves, and hates. He engages in all these activities not as an isolated individual but as a member of overlapping communities which greatly influence his reactions to the classroom experience. To teach the subject matter and ignore the realities of the student's life and the social systems of the college is hopelessly naïve.

There are certain very serious dangers in emphasizing personality development, however. The borderline between facilitation and manipulation is thin. Well-meaning—and not so well-meaning—educators could become so enthused about the developmental approach to higher education that a new kind of paternalism, all the more ugly because it would be hard to recognize, might evolve. But the knowledge contributed by behavioral science is undoubtedly going to be used much more in the designing of higher education in any event, and the only safeguard against manipulation is a clear statement of what the goals and limitations of the development approach ought to be.

Preserving Youthful Idealism

The members of this Committee are deeply concerned about the waning of idealism which occurs during the young adult years. We

6

share an impression, backed up by some empirical data, that the seventeen-year-old is a hesitant, vulnerable idealist with a great reservoir of generosity and an almost equally great tangle of fears and insecurities. The cynicism he displays is—initially at least—merely a cover for his fragile hopefulness. He is concerned about the "big picture," the meaning of life, the improvement of the world, and service to mankind. He is curious, reasonably open, and eager to learn, to have new experiences, to think great thoughts and dream mighty dreams. As the late teen years become the early twenties, he grows more "realistic," becomes aware of the harsh "necessities" of life, and understands that he must "settle down" and "be practical." His intellectual goals and his service-oriented generosity are slowly stifled by the need to compromise with the requirements of the established order. What was wide open, or at least relatively open, at 17 is firmly closed, in most instances, at 22.

This closing off of possibilities and instincts is not caused by the college alone; indeed it probably occurs at a much earlier age among those young people who do not go to college. But the college can and ought to do more to inhibit the closing off process. Currently, there is little in the young person's experience with the college social system that gives him any reason to believe there are alternatives. For this reason, the next major step in higher educational reform must be to look for ways in which the total college experience will preserve for an ever-increasing number of American students their youthful idealism, refined and hardened, perhaps, by the fires of realism, but not burned out.

This clearly is an extraordinarily ambitious goal. It is a vision of social change and reform that is well calculated to overpower the already hard-pressed administrator and faculty member. But this vision, first seen by American higher education itself, is part of a tradition of idealism which is essential to the genius of American higher education. Moreover, to solve the problems that our complex and dynamic society has generated in the last quarter century will require all the idealism we can muster. The preservation of youthful enthusiasm, which we believe now for the first time is technically possible, may no longer be an option but a necessity, and its decline, an unnecessary waste. If this is the case, the argument that such a goal is revolutionary and utopian ceases to be relevant.

The developmental approach to higher education, as will be made clear in a later chapter, is consistent with the goals of the traditional liberal approach. Indeed Nevitt Sanford and John Henry Newman are saying virtually the same thing from different perspectives. American society has determined as a matter of national policy that liberal education is no longer the monopoly of a social elite; but in practice we still limit most of the benefits of such an education to an intellectual elite. Those whose score on I.Q. measures does not exceed 120 are relegated to second—or third, fourth, or fifth—class schools where, in many instances, they receive little more than custodial care until they are dumped on the labor market. Yet this Committee refuses to believe that a much higher proportion of our youth is incapable of systematic thought, unable to break through the bonds of clichés and prejudice and insensitive to the fruits of the Western cultural tradition. We further insist that higher education's responsibility for the developmental needs of our youth will not be discharged until we attempt to discover how, in practice, a liberal education can be possible for Everyman. In the process we might also discover, somewhat to our shock, that by turning our best undergraduate institutions into preparatory academies for the professional graduate schools, we are cheating even the elite of liberal education.

The Tasks of Developmental Education

Intellectual Development

The chief goal of the college and university is to train and develop the human intellect, extending the power of independent and balanced thought and deepening the powers of discrimination and critical expression. But it is no longer possible to take a narrow view of intelligence as "academic knowledge," isolating cognitive growth from moral growth and the general maturation of the person. This view appears untenable not so much for reasons of philosophy, but rather because our knowledge of the nature of the human personality forces us to conclude that cognitive growth which is separated from the development of other aspects of the human personality is illusory or distorted.

Thus the Committee does not take issue with the traditional emphasis of higher education on intellectual development, but it finds most definitions of intellect and most understandings of how it is to be developed far too narrow. To split "intellectual" from "other" development seems highly analytic, for in practice, when dealing with an individual, it becomes virtually impossible to separate intellectual from moral and emotional growth. Or put more precisely, a radical split between the intellectual capacities and the human qualities in an individual would be itself a symptom of a failure of development, which, it is hoped, education—in the broadest sense—would help to resolve. Similarly, the distinction between "intellectual development in the classroom" and "social development in extracurricular activities" seems exceedingly simple. The development of intelligence should occur both because intellectual activities are interesting and exciting in their own right *and* because intellect at its best informs life. Thus that form of intellectual development which has no visible impact on the individual's life, his values, feelings, goals, and deeds, is relatively sterile and undesirable.

Discovering Knowledge

The Committee also rejects the "body of knowledge" tradition of curriculum building. This, in part, is a consequence of the remarkable growth and branching of knowledge, the proliferation of facts, fields, and modes of knowing that makes "coverage of the body" a vain goal. Neither any presumed shape of the body of knowledge nor any current disciplinary categorization should be an indisputable curricular command for all students.

There is a close relationship, however, between the methods that will most engage the student and the methods used to branch out our fields of knowledge, for both involve perception of patterns of relationship, sometimes through conceptual and sometimes through intuitive thinking. This is true for the undergraduate as well as for the most advanced researcher. The process of intellectual discovery may differ only in degree for the freshman and the most distinguished scholar. The curiosity, the playfulness, the search for patterns, the blending of insight with systematic conceptualization are inherent in all intellectual discoveries, whether the explorer is the first one down an untrod path or the thousandth on a tourist route. Learning is essentially discovery, and even though there is now very little of it in American higher education, we can find no reason why discovery should not be returned to the college years. We would even submit that the process of discovery by the individual student ought to be the central tool of higher education.

Teaching to Engage the Student

The teacher, it follows, must be more than a mere transmitter of knowledge (the new teaching machines are at least as effective at this task anyway). The simple reception of knowledge in the eyes and ears of the student is no guarantee of learning. The notion that when knowledge is imparted to a student it will feed his intellect, and his intellect will automatically feed his emotions has been disproved. His intellect and feelings must both be engaged if learning—defined in the classic sense as experience which changes behavior—is to occur. To engage his intellect is not difficult, since classwork is primarily intellectual. To engage his feelings, however, means communicating a relationship to him between the subject matter and the quality of his own life. The task of the teacher is to advance the student's perception of these relationships, to engage him wholly in discovery.

The relationship of teacher and student is a special one, neither parental nor economic. It is a relationship in which an older person assists a younger person in his growth into a mature, wise, competent human being. Knowledge alone is no guarantee of such growth, for growth involves too the forming of values, judgments and commitments, all of which are a part of the life of the man or woman who would be called educated. Values are "caught" rather than taught, and the teacher must communicate to his student the weighing and search for values that are a part of his own life and the life of his subject matter.

What the Student Needs Most

For the majority of students who present themselves at college gates, there exist at least three needs that deserve the utmost attention of the college teacher. First, each student needs to acquire a positive and realistic conception of his own abilities in the world of higher learning and in the world at large. Second, he needs to reach the point of being able to see the structure and interrelations of knowledge so that he may begin the process of forming judgments on his own. Third, he needs to see the relevance of higher learning to the

10

quality of his own life and to see that life in relation to the new kinds of judgments he now makes.

These three developmental tasks are far from being the only ones facing the college-age student, nor are they all the desired tasks of the classroom. They are, rather, very important developmental needs which should be met in a classroom before other tasks are undertaken.

The Crucial Freshman Year

Once a college frees itself from the stricture of a body-of-knowledge curriculum, the possibility opens up of selecting and using knowledge to reach each student's particular intellectual developmental needs. The Freshman year, which is the starting point of a student's higher educational experience, should focus on the interest of each student —what he or she thinks is important. It may be why professors run rats through mazes or how a pollster predicts an election, the meaning of the French Revolution or the reason engines tend to stall in damp weather. In each case the sensitive college would set up classes for groups of students with similar interests to pursue these questions in depth. In these classes the students would not only learn how a psychologist, opinion researcher, historian, or engineer approaches a problem, but also how he resolves it, by acting in the place of the professional himself. Most important, each of the three developmental needs of these freshmen specified above—enhancement of their self-image, an opportunity to form judgments, and relating these judgments to themselves—would be served from the beginning.

This does not mean that all four years of college should be a collection of interest classes. In these years other work, equally difficult and serious, needs to be done to build the student's broader foundation of skills and expertise. The point is that much of what now goes on in these years is the simplest accumulation of facts and credits, and an astonishing percentage of students, even graduates, do not have the least notion of what college is supposed to be about. Equally scandalous is the significant number of students who are becoming higher education's "pushouts," young men and women graciously admitted and then told to take what is offered or leave—and leave is generally what they do. For those who remain, the first semester or year has killed their interest in whatever might follow.

The freshman experience is thus crucial to the college and the student. It is the time when the student's critical attitude toward his studies and college in general is formed, when the college must demonstrate the relevancy of liberal learning to a ready-to-believe but not-yet-convinced student audience. Unfortunately, this is just the time when colleges are most likely to present the least concrete courses taught by the least experienced teachers. The body-of-knowledge theory, with its insistence on progress only from the general to the specific, seems to demand an apprenticeship in generalities (usually of dullness) before the student can progress to anything of personal interest or relevance. And this principle is reinforced by a Puritanical notion that if something might appeal to a young person, it cannot be good for him.

Something better *is* possible when we put the individual student, and not abstract curricular concepts, at the center of the college experience. This is not to suggest a doting, sentimental kind of education, but one which seeks from the beginning the ultimate goal of all liberal education, the shifting of the responsibility for his own education onto the student himself. We seek not simply men who are clever or quick with the answers; we seek men whose skill and expertise is balanced by growth in maturity and wisdom. Such growth is both *possible* and *necessary* for most of the age group now seeking education beyond the high school.

Integrating Campus and Classroom

The out-of-class environment presents highly important opportunities for developmental learning, opportunities at least as strong and influential as those found in the 15 to 18 hours a week spent in the classroom. And since the out-of-class environment is part of the college itself, it should receive the best attention of its educational offices. In this environment the values and attitudes of the classroom must have a high likelihood of finding expression and reinforcement. If the classroom is a place where important matters are discussed or where the search for values goes forward, so too must the campus be. The two must, in fact, be one, demonstrating a consistent relationship that is clear to the student.

The Role of the Peer Group

The most effective teachers usually are other students. While classroom instructors obviously have more knowledge and greater skills

12

than a student's classmates, his classmates interact with him more frequently and at a deeper and more intimate level. They therefore contribute greatly to the level of reception he turns on in the classroom. Just as the friendship group controls production on a factory assembly line and cohesiveness in a military squad, so the student friendship group helps determine what is learned in the college, how it is learned, and what effect both knowledge and the learning experience have on the student's total personality. While our knowledge of how the friendship group can contribute positively to the educational process is still meager, the importance of peer group influence is so obvious that we must rapidly acquire more knowledge of how it works and integrate it into the educational experience—hopefully, without attempting to manipulate it.

Conclusions

The Committee's study of the student in higher education has led it to the following charges, which it offers out of respect for the past achievements of American higher education and with hope for its future achievements.

1. We know that the trauma of leaving home for the first time and entering the relatively impersonal milieu of the college can be severe for young people. But far from attempting to facilitate the transition from home to college, we generally act so as to reinforce the freshman trauma.

2. We also know that the freshman, whatever his faults and weaknesses, generally has an open mind, is eager to work, and willing to learn. Yet our impersonal and mechanical instruction for freshmen seems to extinguish curiosity and to lower intellectual aspirations.

3. Though scholarly research has taught us much about the environmental and developmental circumstances of learning and growth, we largely ignore this knowledge, even in teaching those disciplines which have told us most about the process of human development.

4. Despite the huge sums of money poured into higher education, many, if not most, students are poorly housed, poorly fed, and live in a physical and social environment which is hardly conducive to moral, cultural, or esthetic growth.

5. We measure the worth of our faculty by the distinctions of

the scholars who serve on it. Yet these outstanding scholars are carefully protected from all but the most transitory contact with undergraduates, and teaching in the great universities is left in the hands of inexperienced junior faculty members or assistants, most of whom, for whatever command they have of their professional disciplines, are not trained for classroom instruction.

6. Our basic models for higher education are still aimed at an intellectual elite; our best programs are geared to those whose I.Q.'s are 120 or over. Those of less intelligence are refused admission, filtered out, relegated to inferior schools, or forced to undergo the preprofessional training of the career academician— a training which is of little interest to them and has little to do with the development of any of the qualities liberal education is supposed to promote.

7. Even though we go through the motions of working with student governments, we permit students little real involvement in planning their own education or in shaping the educational environment in which they work and live.

8. We ignore the relevance of education outside the school. The learning forces at work beyond the campus boundaries, the needs of society which affect the students and which they, in turn, can help to serve, are excluded from the curriculum and the life of the university.

9. In our eagerness to train more professional scholars, we are increasingly turning our liberal arts programs into preprofessional academies which demand early specialization and permit little room for free-wheeling, wide-ranging curiosity.

10. Our schools are grimly serious and competitive. The tyranny of the grade point average, the class rank, and the score on the graduate record exam leave little time in the life of the serious student for fun or relaxation. We are then astonished when a student turns to sex or drugs or alcohol or violence as an escape from the academic grind.

11. We do little to help students in their search for commitment, despite our knowledge that they are at precisely the age when commitment is of critical importance. Instead, we stand idly by while young people search fruitlessly for propositions and commitments which will explain the chaos and confusion of life, and worse, we fail to indicate the possibility of a meaningful bridge between the private and the public conscience.

Some of us are more responsible than others for the neglect of the student in American higher education, but all of us must share the responsibility to remedy it. For all the vast and expensive sprawl of American higher education, for all its personnel and capital goods, it is already in serious trouble because of this neglect.

The Committee is calling for something that is very new in American higher education and yet also very old. Our knowledge of the impact of the college as a social and cultural institution on the development of the whole personality of the student is relatively new. But our concern about the student's welfare is as old as the American university. We have become sophisticated enough to realize that rigid rules, minute supervision, and compulsory attendance at church services contribute nothing to the growth of the human personality. Yet the fantastic challenges of the rapid expansion of the last two decades have prevented us from seriously considering whether there are alternative ways in which the college can create a situation which will facilitate the maturation of the young adult without violating his freedom. This report contends that there are indeed such alternatives, and that given the size and complexity of American higher education and the inarticulate restlessness of its student, the alternatives have ceased to be optional.

II

The New Students

IN DISCUSSIONS of the university, the education of students is too often relegated to the end of the list of unsolved problems. And most American universities devote far more attention to every conceivable research question than they do to trying to understand their own students. To be sure, everyone acknowledges that without students there can be no university; and so too, "education" is widely admitted to be one of the functions of a university. Yet the characteristics of students—the fact that they have commitments, aspirations, dreams, needs, psyches, and perhaps souls even *before* being admitted to college—are largely ignored in the concentration on more easily describable features of the university.

Who is the young man or woman who comes to college today? He has been tested, analyzed, studied and speculated about more than any young person in human history, but we still do not understand him very well. All our research does not lead us away from generalizations about the student, his needs, his problems, and his aspirations; it only adds a note of considerable hesitancy to the same generalizations. We know the new student is not the aristocrat or even the fun-loving "big man on campus" of the not so distant past. We know that he is earnest and works hard, that he is frequently worried and anxious, and that his amusements are often frantic or even frenzied. We also know that on occasion he may expend his energies on something as serious as a sit-in or as frivolous as a panty raid. But we are not sure who he is or what he wants, and sometimes it seems that we don't much care.

From the literature we have read and the observations we have made and the experiences we have endured, the members of this Committee feel that at least some assertions can be made about who the student is. To begin with, our student is not one person but many. He is the senior at Harvard who is planning graduate work in nuclear physics and the freshman girl at Michigan State crying softly to herself at night because she is homesick. He is a model of diversity, and he needs many different types of higher educational institutions to serve his diversity. It is not good that every American school, no matter how small or how specialized, aspires to imitate Harvard, for not every student wants or needs a Harvard education.

Some students represent a third or fourth generation of college graduates in their family; others are the first from their ethnic group to venture beyond secondary school. Some are young men with clearly defined career goals, and others are young women who expect college to provide them with a mate. A few are seeking knowledge for its own sake, and others, equally few in number, are interested purely in vocational training. In between lies the majority who are realistic enough to know that a college degree is required for occupational success, but idealistic enough to want to learn something in the process of getting a degree. A few are so brilliant that top-level schools fall over each other competing for them; others are so undistinguished that their schools accept them only because of state laws. The rest, who are the greatest number, are capable of being stimulated to creative thought by challenging ideas and willing, even eager, to learn to think for themselves.

There are some, perhaps as many as ten per cent, who are constricted by serious emotional problems, and there are others, probably even fewer, who are singularly free of such problems. But the majority are at neither extreme, for though they are haunted by self-doubts and insecurity, they can learn their way out of them, if only they meet the right set of circumstances. Some are leftists dedicated to tearing down the established power structure and come to college with sophisticated political skills that cause nightmares for student personnel officials; others are radical rightists dedicated to reestablishing the simplicities of the good old days which never existed. But the greatest number are politically and socially apathetic, ready to make peace with society's demands, yet vaguely resentful because they feel that society is cheating them. Some are extraordinarily sensitive to the artistic and cultural dimensions of life, while the literary taste of others is exhausted by the comic book. However, somewhere in between are the vast majority whose tastes are relatively undeveloped but still relatively unspoiled.

A minority will graduate at the age of 21 after four uninterrupted years at the same college; a majority will be dropouts in some sense, taking many years to finish, transferring from college to college, or never graduating at all. Some few are veterans of the Vietnamese war, and others are doing everything in their power not to be involved in that war. Some are profoundly religious, others convinced agnostics, and still others agonizing through a search for religious meaning. Some commute across the length of the continent, and others merely walk a few blocks to a community college. Some have never been out of the county in which they were born, and others have traveled to the farthest points of the earth. Some aspire to greatness; others are content with a life prospect of moderate mediocrity. Some have had almost as much sexual experience as they claim, and others scarcely know the facts of life.

All of them, wherever they come from, are reflections of the extraordinarily rich, complicated, and nerve-wracking culture that has been built in these United States. If they often feel lost in the contemporary university, it is because they often feel lost in contemporary society. This fact, and all it portends about both university and society, is probably the central fact about American students today. They are enmeshed from kindergarten to the grave in the complex, specialized, bureaucratic, and impersonal institutions of American life. Whether we like it or not, we all—students and teachers alike—live in the most advanced technological nation of the world; and in such a society, as in its educational institutions, individuals tend to feel lost and to look for new ways to assert their individuality and justify their lives.

Perhaps for this very reason these diverse students all have at least one characteristic in common: *They want to learn.* The degree of willingness varies; the ability to learn varies; even the definition of what learning is and the motivation for it varies, but the desire for learning is very much alive when they first arrive on our college campuses.

Beyond this almost universal willingness to learn, several more assertions can be made about many college students. The assertions made in the pages that follow might very well be called characteristics of an elite minority, and the relationship between elites and masses is a question which social science has yet to answer satisfactorily. To state, for example, that the present college scene is characterized by "hippies" is as much an exaggeration as to say that the same scene several years ago was characterized by the "volunteers." The hippies are no more typical of 1967 than the volunteers were of 1962. Changes in the whole student scene proceed very slowly, and differences between the typical students of 15 or 20 years ago and those of today are probably not very great. Nevertheless, the untypical are worth discussing, both because they give color and tone to the university environment and because they are likely to have an influence far greater than their actual number. During the volunteer era, the young people who flocked off to the Peace Corps unquestionably attracted a considerable number of fellow volunteers for work in this country. Similarly, it seems very likely that far more students are inclined to tune out at the present time than those who actually go on LSD trips.

But the most important reason for trying to characterize at some length the new college students is that they present some of the critical problems which educators must respond to. There may be far more of the new students in the multiversities than there are in the state colleges, community colleges, and junior colleges to which more than half of the college population goes. There is unquestionably far more concern about "meaning" at the multiversity than at the junior college. Yet it seems reasonable to assume that the needs for meaning, purpose, community, and love which the multiversity's new student articulates so passionately also exist, if less charged and vocal, in the smaller colleges.

Some Characteristics of the New Student

We can say at least the following about American students:

1. Students are seeking enduring commitments but are skeptical about the ideologies and orthodoxies that clamor for their loyalty.

Anyone who has dealt with college students for any length of time is aware that the quest for meaning, significance, and commitment is stronger than ever before in our students. Young men and women view the chaos, confusion, and disorder in the world around them with profound skepticism. Having experienced neither real peace nor total war, they are disturbed by the chronic disorder of international society. Lacking faith in the inevitability of human progress, they are doubtful about the possibility of a peaceful solution to the nation's racial crisis. Learned in the complexities of the American economy, they cannot side with either participant in a labor-management dispute or in the perennial conflict between liberals and conservatives— of another generation—about the relationship between government and industry. Although they know they need professional competence to earn the material rewards of the good life, they are not convinced that professional careers will yield personal meaning. The more sophisticated find themselves increasingly entertaining the same reservations about romance, marriage, and family. They feel that much is wrong with the world, but they are hard put to articulate clearly what the social ills of mankind are, much less what ought to be done about them or what vision of the good life is possible in contemporary society.

They have no heroes, at least since the death of John Kennedy, and only on occasion can they be moved to turn someone into a villain. Faintly suspicious of the wisdom of their elders—and anyone over 30 is presumed to be irrevocably old—they are sophisticated enough to know that there is little point in blaming elders for the mess they made of the world and less hope of convincing them that it is indeed a mess.

The chaotic disorder of the world today, with the threat of thermonuclear destruction always hovering above it, is enough to dissuade young people from taking the ideologies of the past very seriously or from listening to the advice of a generation responsible for a state close to anarchy. Traditional left-wing ideologies are, for most students, as irrelevant and archaic as the ideologies of the right. Traditional religions hold their own as far as church attendance goes, but are less able to persuade their members to take their cosmogonies seriously as a map of life. Dogmatic ideology is no longer seen as a useful tool with which to face life; articulate social criticism based on a clear vision of what the world ought to be seems largely impossible. Personal witness, direct protest, insistence on the importance of the interpersonal, the authentic, and the genuine are replacing systematic ideologies as a basis of action among substantial numbers of students.

The new college student therefore would *like* to be able to believe in something or someone, but as a matter of principle virtually rejects the possibility. He is not incapable of commitment or conviction, but his sales resistance is very strong.

2. Because of their suspicion about formal ideology, the new students turn to human relationships as the source of most of the purpose and meaning they seek in their lives.

The student leftist who when queried about the nature of his ideology replied, "Our ideology is Love," spoke for his whole generation; and the hippies with their demand for "flower power" represent in caricature the kind of honest, open, trusting, and undemanding relationships the student thinks will be the key to personal happiness. Man has always wanted to love and be loved, but the explicit, self-conscious, and agonized pursuit of love as a rationale for existence has not been so much a part of Western culture since the age of the medieval troubadors. Unfortunately, love is easy to talk about and more difficult to practice. For all their ability to quote from the *Art of Loving,* most students are only remotely conscious of the need for self-sacrifice and self-discipline in the love relationship. To speak of love which is "spontaneous" and "makes no demands" is to describe a relationship which is necessarily transitory and unreal, since once love goes beyond the initial stage of infatuation, it must be reflective and must make demands. An ideology based on love may produce brilliantly mystical rhetoric, but it is a poor basis on which to attempt to organize either a total society or a small group within society. Since most young adults are only beginning to learn the "art of loving," their adoption of an ideology of love is bound to lead to disappointment and frustration.

3. The contemporary college student feels strongly the need to belong but is profoundly skeptical about most of the organizations he encounters, particularly an organization that claims to offer him an education.

Ever since Western man left behind the warmth, intimacy, and social support of the rural village, he has striven to create within

21

the industrial metropolis a community structure with some of the merits of the old folk society. On the whole, Western man shows little more than poetic regret over the loss of bucolic joys of the past; for him, the affluence and comfort of modern life have been worth the price. Nonetheless, it has been his dream through the years of migration to the metropolis that he could have his cake and eat it too, that he could by some kind of free contract reestablish the tribe in the metropolis. Until very recently, this quest for community had been a conscious quest for only a few. But among the younger generation the search for meaningful group relationships has become quite explicit. "Belonging," "participating," "sharing," and the skills they demand are, for the generation currently going through colleges and universities, among the most important goals of human existence. The desire to belong, to be part of an intimate fellowship, and to serve others in a face-to-face community seems to be more articulate and more dominant than ever before. Nor should we be surprised that a generation reared on Freud, Kafka, Kierkegaard and Camus in the apartments and Levittowns of modern America is deeply anxious over its search for belonging, its needs for roots.

Despite all his enthusiasm about belonging, the new college student is anything but impressed by the organizations which he might join. He looks at the big university, the big government, big business, big labor, the big research enterprise, and the big church with considerable dismay, and asks with a mixture of Martin Buber and Soren Kierkegaard, "Where in all this bigness and impersonality is there room for my lonely suffering soul; where can I find a meaningful I-Thou dialogue?"

The new college student wants solidarity, participation and fellowship unequivocally and passionately. But he views most organizations of our computerized, bureaucratized, rationalized, formalized, urban industrial society as almost by their nature inimical to the freedom and spontaneity of the human spirit. The organized society can be cold, heartless, and impersonal. It can turn you into a cog in the machine, an IBM card processed through a computer. One must, of course, make one's peace with organizations, and students are usually prepared to concede in theory that organizations are necessary for pooling human resources and that without a division of labor, modern society would be impossible. But in practice many of the organizations with which they come in contact seem subtly depersonalizing; few provide any real community.

22

4. The new student is generous and idealistic in his own fashion but is frequently fearful that any long-term commitment to social service may destroy his idealism and thwart his freedom.

While much of the student population remains apathetic and it is difficult to compare the idealism of one generation with that of another, the spectacular growth of volunteer movements is striking evidence of the extraordinary generosity and enthusiasm in today's students, if touched by the right kind of appeal uttered by the right kind of person. Whether the volunteer era will continue and whether it will have a substantial impact on American society is not yet clear, but it is clear that the college has generally ignored the marvelous opportunities for integrating education and life that the volunteer movements provided. From the point of view of the youthful volunteers who have served in their country and abroad, however, the critical question is not whether the volunteer movement will continue, but whether in fact it has any meaning.

The volunteer very quickly discovers that the love and service he wishes to bring to his fellow men is not always warmly received and may be quite inadquate. Worse still, he may learn that two years of hard work and enthusiastic commitment have only a marginal effect on the social evils he has dedicated himself to eliminate. He apparently has the alternative of withdrawing from active social reform into some relatively secure domain where his generosity and idealism will not be contaminated by the mess and exhaustion of social action (like a career in higher education), or of acquiring the skills that are required for social action and committing himself to a long period, perhaps a lifetime, of grueling and frequently dissatisfying efforts to correct the causes of social distress. The volunteer realizes all too well that such a commitment will plunge him into a world of uncertainty and ambiguity, where frequent compromise is necessary and where he runs the risk of sacrificing his ideals for the sake of getting something done. It sometimes seems preferable to be an alienated radical critic than to run the risk of being an involved but compromising activist.

5. The new students, for all their apparent poise and sophistication, are frequently hesitant and uncertain.

Their self-distrust and self-suspicion make them vulnerable to self-hatred and on occasion despair. Middle class and particularly upper middle class society in the United States continues to stress achievement as much as ever, although currently achievement is measured by more subtle indicators than annual income. The young person who has arrived at college has already passed through a series of rankings, evaluations, and comparisons with his fellow students and knows full well that such rankings will continue until the day he dies. Since successful and skillful performance is expected relatively early in life, and since reward is contingent on performance, it is rare for a middle class youth to experience unconditional acceptance in the course of his growing up. Under such circumstances self-doubt, self-rejection, self-hatred, and self-punishment become almost endemic to the collegiate culture. Feelings of rejection and worthlessness, although they may be obscured by a veneer of poise and sophistication, occasionally incapacitate the student and frequently impair his real abilities. With greater or lesser vigor, the new college student hates and fears the rankings, evaluations, the comparisons, the gradings, of the higher educational system. But he is inclined to concede ruefully that there is not much he can do about it and that it is a good preparation for what he has to face the rest of his life.

6. Because of his doubts about himself, about organizations, and the possibility of faith and commitments, the new college student has a tendency to be suspicious and distrustful of the administration, and to a lesser extent, the faculty of his college.

The college is the most obvious manifestation of the organized society. The school and its officers become ink blots into which the students can project their frustrations, not only with the college experience, but also with the larger society. Most students will not attack the president in the school paper; they will not picket the administration building; they will not call the school officers obscene names or caricature them on placards. But they will be deeply suspicious in their relationships with the representatives of the college administration, whether they are personnel officers, clerks, secretaries, or campus police. The student's relationships with faculty are apt to be somewhat less resentful, if only because through sheer frequency of exposure he gets to know a little more about his teachers and at least on occasion has a meaningful, if fleeting, relationship with a few. The large number of college students who aspire to careers in professional Academia is an indication of the relatively

24

good image that the college professor has been able to maintain among his students. That the image remains so untarnished is an interesting commentary on the naïveté of the students, most of whom apparently do not realize that the organization and goals of the academic guilds are among the principal reasons for their own disadvantaged position in the college.

7. Students come to college with a great deal of excitement and willingness to do the work demanded of them, but their expectations and performance usually decline very rapidly during the first months of the freshman year.

Incoming students expect the college years to be exciting and challenging, both intellectually and socially; they are eager for this new adventure in their life. Almost as quickly as their expectations about work fade, so do their expectations about the excitement and challenge of higher education. Students learn that college is rather like high school, that most of what one does is still "Mickey Mouse," and that boredom and dullness are just as prevalent in college. Most teachers are uninteresting and many are uninterested. Course requirements frequently seem to be make-work, and programs of study appear to have little connection with career goals, personal concerns, or intellectual curiosity. As a practiced expert in the game of making peace with the system, the student soon adjusts his needs and expectations to fit its requirements. At the end of four years, he even has a certain loyalty to his college. To be sure, it has not provided what he hoped it would as a freshman, but at least it has furnished him with the degree that is a prerequisite for employment or for further education, has offered social diversions to vary the routine, perhaps has found him a spouse, and has enabled him to prolong his youth—and his entry into the System—a bit longer than would otherwise have been possible.

8. Most students apparently expect that the college years will mark the definitive end of their dependence on their parents.

Even those who do not live away from home anticipate that college will provide the environment necessary for them to acquire the independence, initiative, and sense of responsibility that are expected of adults. The final breaking of family ties, especially when postponed as in American society, is bound to be a painful and ambivalent experience, filled with a yearning for adulthood and at the same time a regret for the loss of childhood. Since the break only becomes possible when a sufficient sense of selfhood has evolved, many students enter college ill-prepared to depart from the confines of their family, however eager to do so they may be.

Profile of the New Student

The background, the needs, the abilities, and the aspirations of the student entering college today are as diverse as the complex country which gave him birth. The great variety in American higher education reflects the equal variety in American culture. But there are some constants. Most students are curious, eager to learn, and willing to work, though they may not understand fully what learning is or what higher education is supposed to be for. They are seeking a meaningful explanation of the complex phenomena of life. They are also looking for a system of intimate relationships that will provide the dimension of belonging, which seems to them such a crucial part of life. Their generosity may lack depth and sophistication, but it has also produced volunteer movements the like of which the nation has never seen. They are afraid that they are not tough enough or ruthless enough to succeed in the competitive game that is required for success in American society. They are puzzled about who they are and whether they can be strong enough to stand on their own two feet, independent of parental support. Suspicious of the irrationality and corruption of adult society, they are, nevertheless, willing to make a deal with it since they see no feasible alternatives. Like all young people, they are immensely interested in and concerned about sex and expect that the college years will provide an opportunity for considerable sexual experimentation. The new students may also vaguely expect to have a good time in college, but they quickly adjust to a style of life which permits good times only as a periodic escape from the deadly serious business of classroom competition and achievement.

From the point of view therefore of someone seriously interested in education, the students of the midsixties are a mixed bag. They are too rebellious to expect to learn from the wisdom of those who have gone before them, and yet most of them are too docile to contemplate serious revolt. They are curious, open and willing to work, but all too ready to make their peace with the system when they realize that it places little dividend on intellectual adventuresomeness. For all their weaknesses and ambivalences, however, their intelligence, curiosity, and capacity for work certainly ought to provide the educator with an extraordinary challenge. Unfortunately, most educators have little time to recognize or consider these qualities, much less to speculate on how educational programs might be developed to serve and strengthen them.

III

The New Students
Go To College

WHEN MILLIONS of freshmen flock through the gates of their college each September, they find that the school of their choice has a whole series of policies and structures designed to ward off the annual student invasion. The more perceptive students soon come to the conclusion that their personalities and expectations are of little concern to the college. What is important is that the students behave as required so that the college can achieve its own goals of survival and expansion, and the primacy of these goals means that the education of the students has rather low priority.

Admissions Policy: Upgrade the Student Body

As the college views its seventeen- and eighteen-year-old charges on the first day of their freshman year, the most critical question it asks is whether these students are brighter than last year's, for it is the unquestioned aim of almost every American college and university to upgrade the quality of its student body. If you are getting better students, then you are getting better as a college, and if the quality of your students is remaining fixed or, heaven forbid, is slipping, then your school is in serious danger.

How does a college determine whether this year's students are better than the last lot? By relatively simple measuring sticks, with an assist from recruiters. The most widely used yardstick is the cutting point on the national College Entrance Examination Board (CEEB) score. If the average score of the new freshman class is higher than it was last year, then the student body is better. And if young people who were admitted last year could not have made it now, then clearly the quality of the student body has improved. The higher the median CEEB score, the happier administrators and faculty members are, because a high cutting point indicates that the less intelligent adolescents have been filtered out and the school is getting only the most promising ones.

The usual college policy of academic upgrading assumes, but rarely states, that only a certain percentage of high school graduates are capable of further education, at least in the respectable colleges and universities. It also assumes that many of the students who are per-force admitted into colleges and universities at the present time do not fall within the elite that is bright enough—as measured by the CEEB exams—to be worth the efforts of a college. Fortunately for the college, the tremendous size of the cohorts advancing on it enables many schools to define the educable elite as a smaller and smaller proportion of the total without any decline in the actual number enrolled in respectable schools. The rest of the legions are relegated to institutions where they will receive, despite fancy jargon used to obscure the fact, custodial care. By careful counseling a few of them, it is alleged, will be salvaged for later entrance into the more respectable institutions. Others will be "cooled out" of higher education altogether. Still others may struggle through and obtain some sort of A.A. or A.B. degree as a consolation prize, but it will fool no knowledgeable person as to the quality or utility of the education they received.

If an institution is required by state law to admit large numbers of young people it considers uneducable—and often it seems that anyone with an I.Q. under 120 is deemed to belong in such a group —the most favored way of getting around this threat to its academic rise is to select out this group in the first semester of the freshman year. The selecting out is accomplished largely through teaching assistants who are delegated the grim task of eliminating the unfit by enforcing tough standards. In some multiversities the freshman composition course is the favorite execution site for those that the school does not want around its campus at the end of the first semester. There is no need, of course, for the university to count the cost in human suffering or in wasted human talent of such a policy.

Rarely does one hear doubts that the homogeneous schools are good, both humanly and educationally. It is usually taken for granted that all high CEEB scorers should be put in one kind of educational institution and all dullards in other institutions. No one seems to question whether the elite should be isolated from the rest of society and be persuaded of its own elitism even before it has accomplished anything save high entrance examination scores. It is even less questionable whether society should relegate all those who have been defined as "also rans" at the age of 17 to other institutions, which already marks them, no matter how comfortably they may be able to live, as failures. Whatever the human and social costs of this division of higher educational labor, the decision has been made that the demands of a technological society for highly competent experts can most efficiently be served by segregating the intelligent from the dumb.

Even though periodic lip service is paid to the contrary proposition, it is agreed that for all practical purposes a talent for higher education, as well as the kinds of abilities which can contribute to the health and welfare of society, can be measured by standardized tests. That some young people have a marvelous test sense but are not very creative or expressive, is not considered relevant. Nor does it matter much that the emphasis on performance in standardized tests turns them into objects of horror which wreak considerable havoc in the young adult world and quite conceivably frighten the more sensitive, and hence more promising, students into far poorer performances than what they are really capable of, or that the kind of mastery of data required to score impressively on such tests may have nothing to do with higher learning, at least as this concept has traditionally been understood in the Western educational tradition.

American colleges are caught in a paradox which says that everyone has the right to higher education and affirms at the same time that society has special needs for those who are most able and most competent. The compromise solution is that the able are given what educators consider a good education, and the less able are given a poor education. However, an outside observer might note that the able are actually likely to receive a poor education and the less able no education at all—even if they do spend four years on a college campus.

Freshman Orientation

The main goal of the freshman orientation period—usually lasting a week, which is in itself an interesting commentary on how important it is considered—is to fit the new student into the day-to-day operation of the school as quickly and as smoothly as possible. Orientation is designed to teach him the basic geographic and academic maps needed to survive in the college, and the behavior expected of him. The freshman learns what services are really available, where the important offices are, which rules will be enforced, and what academic requirements will be imposed. If he feels lonely in the future, he knows where the counseling center is, if there *is* a counseling center. If he becomes ill, orientation has taught him where to find the student health services. If he has trouble in his studies, his guide should be his academic advisor. If his religious faith is troubled, he has learned where the campus chaplains are. He also knows where the book store, the laundry, the post office, and other indispensable agencies are located. Once these landmarks have been mapped out, he is ushered into lecture halls and turned over to the tender mercies of the teaching assistants, where he is expected, both academically and humanly, to sink or swim by himself. If he is caught breaking the rules, he cannot plead ignorance. At the end of orientation administrators can, with a sigh of relief, assure themselves that they have integrated a new freshman class into their campus milieu and return to the more important tasks to which higher educational administrators devote their time.

Freshmen are clearly expected to assimilate themselves to the ongoing system as quickly as possible; the college need not do anything special to maintain their curiosity, stimulate their interest, or expose them to intellectual experiences. These things are thought to take place almost automatically in the classroom. Pompous and generally incoherent discourses by nervous assistant deans are generally taken as a sufficient introduction to the riches of the Western intellectual tradition.

After the brief orientation period is over, freshmen must settle down to the very serious task of mastering their subject matter. If they have adjustment problems, the counseling services are expected to take care of them, particularly if the problems should happen to impair their mastery of the subject matter as reflected in midterm grades. No particularly close connection is seen between the developmental needs of the young adult and the cognitive aspects of his education. The classroom takes care of the cognitive, and the student health service takes care of the other dimensions of his life, with perhaps some small residue left over for the campus chaplains. The professor is not supposed to be a psychotherapist, and it is not at all necessary that he be psychologically sophisticated, even if he is teaching courses in psychology. The personal problems of the student are his own problems, not the professor's. The instructor who takes too much interest in his students' personal problems is very likely to be warned that such an investment of energy could interfere with the progress of his academic career. Once orientation week is over, it is high time for freshmen to begin to prepare for graduate school.

It would seem therefore that the college's major expectation of freshman orientation is to fit the new students in the college in such an efficient and expeditious way that the transition through which the freshmen are going from secondary school to college and from home to campus dormitory will create as little trouble as possible for the college and its administrators and faculty. So long as the young people's developmental needs do not get in the way, they are of small concern to the school. The quicker the freshman can turn his attention to preparing for the first semester examinations, the better. When research scholars appear on the scene and suggest that in the instant socialization process most intellectual curiosity is effectively destroyed, their colleagues on the faculty and administration pretend not to be listening.

Upgrading the Faculty

Just as every school worth its salt is trying to upgrade the quality of its student body, so a school that is on the make must improve its faculty, pushing its position in the academic social register a little higher. The school that has made it must constantly seek new and better faculty members so that it will not be overtaken by some ambitious noveau riche state university. In other words, colleges and universities are competing with each other so that the next time the

American Council of Education attempts a replication of the Cartter report, more of their departments will receive favorable mention.

The process of upgrading the faculty is quite involved. It begins by attracting more distinguished faculty members. Distinguished faculty members are those whom members of their discipline say are distinguished. Their distinction is measured by how many publications they have produced (at times no matter how trivial or irrelevant or how inappropriate frequent publication is in a particular discipline), by the reputation of the graduate school they attended (which, in turn, depends on how distinguished its faculty was), and by the ardency with which they subscribe to the current professional orthodoxies or, even better, the approved unorthodoxies. Finally, after all these requirements are met, a faculty member still is not really considered distinguished unless he is known by people who already have distinguished reputations and he also knows a sufficient number of other distinguished people.

How does a school go about collecting these prestigious faculty members, especially at a time when there are far more positions available for such men than there are candidates to fill them? There are three sure ways: First of all, the distinguished academician must be promised a high salary, a large number of fringe benefits, and an almost unlimited opportunity for other kinds of employment which will increase his annual income even more. Second, he must be promised a light teaching load. In fact the more distinguished he is, the lighter his teaching load must be, so it is quite possible that the most distinguished faculty members will be hired to teach absolutely nothing at all. Third, he must be promised that most, if not all, of the time he does spend in the classroom will be with graduate students. There are several unique advantages of teaching graduate students when compared with undergraduates, the most important of which is that the docile graduate student is more likely to work *for you,* whereas the pesty undergraduate is more likely to demand that you work *for him.* When such a renowned academician has received his high salary, his light teaching load, and his coterie of promising graduate students, he can proceed with enthusiasm and vigor to do more research and to develop an even bigger reputation than he has, and thus improve the reputation of the faculty on which he is serving until the day comes when another institution offers him more attractive working conditions.

33

Given the present shortage of distinguished scholars, the academic marketplace is definitely a seller's preserve, and the new academic freebooter is a highly mobile man who can dictate his own terms and limit his interests to his own career and the requirements of his profession. He need not display much loyalty either to his school or to its students. He is certainly not expected to waste his time with the noisy, unwashed horde of undergraduates for whose education inexperienced teaching assistants are paid enough money to keep them alive—until the blessed day when they too can begin to compete for the riches and the glories that come from being a distinguished professor.

Obviously, not every school can have as distinguished a faculty as Harvard or Berkeley, but at least it can try to imitate them as far as its resources permit. If it cannot follow all the norms that Mother Harvard uses in choosing its faculty members, it can do its best to use some of these norms, bent a little, if necessary, to develop its own brand of quality. Under such circumstances the undergraduates, for whom presumably the school came into existence, are taught by undistinguished faculty—many of whom turn out to be good teachers, thus frustrating the basic premise of the system that no talent should be wasted on undergraduates—or by teaching assistants who are serving out their time with undergraduates until they can get the prized union card which admits them as full-fledged members of the academic guilds.

We salve our conscience over the use of teaching assistants—in some multiversities the majority of courses are taught by teaching assistants—with the argument that since these instructors are young and relatively close to the undergraduates in age, they are frequently far better teachers than are distinguished faculty members. There is little or no evidence to substantiate this self-serving claim, and there are a number of reasons for thinking that it is quite erroneous. The teaching assistant is a journeyman in his profession, and like all people who are new in a field, he can be more inflexible and hyper-professional than a master of the art. In his enthusiasm for high academic standards—which he, like most other people, interprets to mean more hard work—the junior-grade professional is often supercilious and demanding in his relationship with his students. And because he is still quite young, he is usually relatively unskilled in human relations and lacks the maturity and wisdom one might expect of those who deal with students just entering the critical years of their intellectual development. The teaching assistant is also busy doing his own course work and his thesis. This leaves him little time to put serious effort into the preparation of his class material, much less into correcting papers or establishing any personal communication with his students. Finally, many teaching assistants are newly married and find that with the great pressures of their academic responsibilities, marriage adjustment can be extraordinarily difficult, particularly if both partners are pursuing the almighty Ph.D.

It is therefore not particularly reasonable to expect high-quality teaching from assistants, and not many people seriously argue that we get it. But there doesn't seem to be any other solution to the twin problems of providing someone who will deal with the hordes of undergraduates and of finding some source of income to keep graduate students from starvation before they get their advanced degrees. The academic marketplace is ruled by harsh economic laws. There are plenty of students and a considerable number of potential teaching assistants, but few distinguished faculty members. Thus the faculty member is usually able to write his own ticket, and the student is constrained to take what he gets and like it. His only choice is to take it or leave it; most do, in fact, leave it—only two out of every five freshmen can stand four uninterrupted years at the same college.

Designing a Curriculum

One of the great indoor sports of American faculties is fiddling with the curriculum. The faculty can engage in interminable arguments during years of committee meetings about depth versus breadth. They can fight almost without end about whether education should be providing useful or liberal knowledge. They can write learned books and articles about the difficulties of integrating human knowledge at the time of a knowledge explosion. And of course the battle between general and special education is likely to go on until the end of time. Curricula are constantly being changed. New courses are introduced, new programs are offered, new departments are created (to quickly become powerful vested interests of their own), sequences of courses are rearranged, honors programs are introduced, catalogues are rewritten, teaching loads are adjusted, and a grand and glorious time is had by all.

The harsh truth is that all this activity is generally a waste of

35

time as far as providing better education for students is concerned. There is no evidence to date that young people learn any more or any less, no matter how their academic curriculum is arranged. The controversy over curriculum gives the faculty something to do and serves their need for neatness and elegance. But since all the emphasis is on the subject matter and the disciplines that are considered necessary for higher education, and practically no emphasis is on the needs of the students, curriculum reform is invariably carried on in a psychological vacuum.

The term "experimental college" all too frequently means merely a college with a very flexible curriculum. It is the central contention of this report that experiments which do not take into account the personality development of the student are bound to fail. For curricular reform to be effective, it must have as its primary reference point the student and his developing personality. It is interesting to speculate on what model of man many of the more ingenious and elaborate proposals for curriculum reform are based. Many of these proposals leave the impression that the student is a first cousin of Adam Smith's economic man—a rational, passive absorber of information.

In the interminable discussion over curriculum reform, there seems to be little recognition of the fact that if the curriculum is to be really effective educationally, the material presented in the classroom must be related to the needs and interests of the students. Or in plain English, a teacher has to start from where the students are. A frequent argument voiced by academicians is that their principal concern is with subject matter. They teach their own disciplines and cannot be psychotherapists. It apparently follows that the faculty members' job is to present their subject matter whether the students are listening or not, and the question of whether they are able to listen does not even arise. This narrow focus on subject matter leads to certain assumptions in curriculum design, and most of the curricula of our colleges today, reformed or not, are based on these assumptions:

1. The first two years of higher education should be concerned with general elements of learning and the final two years with more concentrated and specialized efforts.

2. College courses are essentially preprofessional training. Hence during the years of general education a highly watered down

summary of many disciplines is presented to students, while during the last two years a few disciplines are laid out to dry.

3. The information and skills which must be mastered to enter the company of the learned can be broken down into the categories of the various academic disciplines.

4. Since there is so much to learn and since the disciplines of the guilds are so complex, it is absolutely necessary to spend half of the working week in the classroom absorbing the knowledge that the guild representative makes available.

5. The student's mastery of the various disciplines can be measured by a scale of grades which purport to rank his performance on tests and term papers, and the more standardized the marking procedure, the better. The professor is expected to be able to gauge this mastery of the discipline without knowing anything about the student besides what he puts in the examination blue book or in his term paper.

6. Fitness for graduate training in an academic discipline, which is the only *real* professional training, can be adequately predicted from the grades an undergraduate receives.

7. Therefore a student would be ill-advised to experiment in matters outside those deemed important by the particular guild he wishes to enter. There is not much room for adventure in lower division courses, but experimentation is even riskier in upper division courses. It might cause a promising student to miss a course that is required for admission to his chosen guild, or it might lower his grade average, which could keep him out of graduate school.

What Aristotle, Plato, John Henry Newman, or John Dewey would say about these assumptions concerning curriculum is problematic. But then the first three, and probably even the fourth, would hardly qualify for appointment to any of our more distinguished faculties today.

Teaching the Curriculum

What is charitably called teaching in higher education is based on these beliefs:

1. A vast amount of knowledge must be imparted during the course of a student's four years in college. This knowledge is available in textbooks, anthologies, and lectures, disseminated on

a mass production basis. The assembly line is checked by instructors a few hours each week in the classroom and perhaps one extra hour a week in their offices.

2. Information must be imparted as professionally as possible, so students are treated to predigested versions of past discoveries and controversies within a given discipline and only rarely hear of current events that affect the discipline.

3. The most effective teacher is one who demands the most hours of the hardest work from the student. The good teacher therefore has very stern requirements about the amount of reading and writing and very high expectations about the mastery of the information and the jargon of his own discipline. And to maintain these high standards, he must rigorously ignore the personal growth of his students. It is an article of faith that at least the cognitive dimension of the student's personality will develop if he exhausts himself on the traditional bibliography and term paper before the end of the semester.

4. Only after several years of ingesting this information and reproducing it on demand is a student capable of thinking for himself, and only then is he ready for individual work or participation in a small seminar. At that point too, he can be permitted the reward of a brief, fleeting contact with a distinguished senior member of the faculty.

5. For this reason, freshmen are kept out of seminars and seniors are put in seminars, despite the fact that both the needs and the style of most seventeen-year-olds are more suited to the seminar, and if anybody is able to tolerate the lecture hall, it should be the senior.

6. The most intelligent and gifted students are provided with more of exactly the same instruction that the average student receives, but they are expected to master more information and jargon and write more papers and bibliographies. This is a great favor to them because it will give them a headstart when they get into graduate school.

7. The less gifted students get less of the standard treatment and are expected to produce a little less—they need not write as many term papers, read quite so many books, or display such a mastery of jargon and information. However, once their performance falls

below a certain level, it is clear that they do not belong in college, and must gently but firmly be cooled out.

The Organization of the University

The tacit assumption made by the faculty and administration in organizing the college or university is that students are, by and large, simple-minded savages who will destroy the peace, order, and reputation of a school if they are not controlled and kept at bay. As a result, despite some external differences, the organizational structure of many modern higher educational institutions is not terribly different from that of penal institutions, with the single important exception that a student is relatively free to leave the college or university. The students' lives, however, are governed by regulations which they have had no share in forming and generally no participation in enforcing. The premise behind this exclusion of students from the real governance of their lives is that they are not mature enough to be trusted with the responsibility. The social structure of the school is designed to keep the student away from the important people on campus unless it is absolutely imperative that he talk to them. Thus it is very difficult for him to establish a relationship with the dean or even an assistant dean, and probably more difficult to get to see his instructors except at certain specified and quite limited periods of the week. The premise behind this calculated social distance is that those who control the institution's charges are too important to be bothered and will never get their work done if they are.

The procedures and style of the university or college are calculated to prevent students from creating problems for the institution by expressing their own individuality within it. As a result, faculty and administrators do all they can in their dealings with students to standardize procedures and depersonalize contacts. If too much room were permitted for idiosyncratic problems or too much tolerance for personality differences, the organizational efficiency of the school would deteriorate. Thus for all the lip service paid to personal development in the catalogue, the actual practice in most colleges is to keep matters as impersonal as possible.

Those agents of the institution with whom the students are in most frequent contact—secretaries, clerks, tellers in the bursar's office, and campus police—are frequently people who, perhaps with very good

39

reason, do not particularly like young people and are quite successful at generating a reciprocal dislike of themselves. The principal role of these functionaries is to serve as a buffer between the students and the administrators and faculty, and they often seem to take delight in frustrating and degrading students.

The housing and food services of a college or university are part of the impersonal style. They have no educational function; they are essentially profit-making or at least self-amortizing enterprises. A dormitory or lunchroom will preferably make money, or at least not seriously endanger the prospect of amortization, so comforts, frills, and niceties are kept to a bare minimum. This has led to a tremendous expansion of urban renewal-type dormitories and food services whose best efforts compare unfavorably with those of the military establishment. In these projects, of course, there is no room for graceful living, much less for the evolution of small, intimate communities.

In college, students are thrown into huge building complexes, where their own rooms are rather small and barrack-like and inhabited by several other people. Often the expression of personality through furniture or decorations is severely restricted. Functional desks and beds are cramped together, and the rules proclaim that there is to be no painting, not even a thumbtack on the wall. This kind of communal living is thoroughly "un-American," outside of the army. The students are isolated from people other than those of their own age and sex; there are no adults, no children, not even pets. This situation is actually very much like what Plato recommends when he proposes that to have people become fit for his own state and freed from the conditioning of a previous corrupt society, the young be segregated from their parents for a period and be raised in isolation outside of the city. The conditions would lend themselves nicely for brainwashing.

But nobody is really much interested in obtaining control, so the net effect is more one of omission. Students live together in uneasy proximity without reaping a commensurate benefit in the development of deeper relations. Many students long for more privacy, and they find themselves unable to cope with the intrusions and the noise of so many strangers. Sometimes a restrictive and narrowminded director or other supervisor adds to their annoyance. But students tend to be good boys and girls. Griping and an occasional raid on the kitchen or a food fight seem to satisfy their need of protest. There has been a tendency in recent years to give up building large complexes. Many schools and hospitals are no longer the forbidding huge armories we have been used to since the turn of the century. Colleges, however, have been continuing to build, though not everywhere, large structures. The pressure of increasing enrollment is one reason. But we will need to give much more attention to how our living arrangements can further, differently for different students, both sociability and privacy.

Since the famous research of Elton Mayo almost 40 years ago, virtually every educated American has become aware that informal, face-to-face human groups not only exist in the midst of large, formal, bureaucratic organizations, but also are the cement which holds the formal organization together and a major determinant of its effectiveness. It has not yet dawned on many American educators, however, that if an informal group is of maximum importance to the factory and the military establishment, it is of equal importance to the college. Nor do educators realize that students learn far more out of the classroom than in it—when they are with their fellow students rather than their teachers—and that their friendships will either draw them in or out of the organization around them. Yet research indicates that most friendship cliques do anything but facilitate the goals of the formal college organization.

The admissions policy, the freshman orientation program, the selection of teachers, the designing of a curriculum and classroom instruction, and the social and physical organization of a typical American college or university pay little attention to the needs and problems of students and the development of the students' personalities. It is hard to escape the conclusion that so long as the students don't sully the public image of their colleges, American higher education really doesn't much care what happens to its undergraduates.

IV

A College For
The New Student

THIS REPORT HAS two related themes, which were discussed in the previous chapters: 1) the college is a major influence on the development of the student's personality and must therefore assume responsibility for the quality and direction of this development; 2) even the college's central task of guiding the intellect cannot be done well unless the school realizes that the acquisition of knowledge takes place in a context of emergent adulthood. Recognition of these facts does not mean merely that the college must assume a new responsibility, but we would argue that it ought to meet a unique opportunity—an opportunity to participate in the emotional growth of its young students and to integrate this growth with formal education. A college that succeeded in both would make education far more effective and useful than ever before.

It is difficult to specify exactly what the college ought to do, since we are only beginning to understand the possibilities of developmental* education; but even if our understanding were much more sophisticated, *a priori* schemes would not be of much help. At this time it seems wiser to suggest certain areas in which fruitful experimentation can occur, with the hope that these experiments will be

*For simplicity, the Committee has chosen the word "developmental" to describe a college experience which integrates the student's cognitive development and the development of his whole personality. A more precise but cumbersome label would be Nevitt Sanford's "education for individual development."

the first steps toward instituting developmental education in our colleges.

Understanding the Student and His Needs

The most unique feature of the undergraduate experience is that it coincides with a critical stage in the life of a young person—the transition into adulthood. It is also an advantage for a college that its attempt to form a liberally educated man comes at the time when the man himself is being formed. The student knows he comes to college as an adolescent, that he will leave as an adult, and that there is a difference between the two which he is supposed to discover while in college. This difference is presumed to include new attitudes, tastes, values, commitments, and competencies, which the college is supposed to foster.

Our understanding of the development of the young adult is neither theoretically unassailable nor empirically grounded. Our ignorance about the emergence of the human adult is considerably greater than our knowledge. But there are some things we *do* know, and on the basis of our present knowledge of the developmental process, it is clear not only what many mistakes are being made in higher education, but also that there are at least some ways of undoing these mistakes.

It is not the purpose of this report to present a detailed theory of personality, but, using the terms of Erik Erikson, we can say that since college spans the years of late adolescence to young adulthood, it is a time when the young person is seeking identity and intimacy. The boundaries of the core of the personality are being firmed up, and a young person is striving to determine in broad outline who he is, what his major goals are in life, and what meanings he can derive from the various experiences that touch him as he moves through life. As he passes from a period of identifications to a period of identity, he must be free to act on his own. His physical and intellectual capacities must be challenged, and he must acquire skills that will enable him to respond to challenge with confidence. He must be tested to the limits of his resources so that he knows how far he can go without straining his abilities. Only by testing his limitations and competencies can he feel sure that the self which he is simultaneously discovering and fashioning is capable of facing the rest of life with any hope of experiencing significant success.

43

With mastery of the identity crisis, there is another and equally serious crisis which, curiously enough, has yet to find its way into the jargon of the college student—the crisis of intimacy. The young student must learn to comunicate with others, both verbally and in writing, and even more important, in deed. He must face the often lonely challenge of giving himself to others in trust, and the even more frightening challenge of receiving others when they give themselves to him in trust. He must respond to his own altruistic instincts enough to fight the temptation toward cynicism. As Nevitt Sanford has said, "Possibly the only cure for self-contempt is an actual experience of being helpful." Finally, and most important, the student must become convinced that he can love and is worthy of being loved. To say that the college student is seeking identity and intimacy is perhaps merely restating something that is obvious to anyone who deals with young people. Nonetheless, American higher education has failed to recognize explicitly that cognitive development which is not integrated into the quest for identity and intimacy deals only with a fraction of the human personality and that this fraction is necessarily of secondary importance to the young person arriving at chronological adulthood.

The fact that certain of the college's intellectual requirements also are developmental needs is well illustrated in freshman composition courses. To the college, very frequently the "comp" program is an achievement hurdle for the freshman to clear—or leave. The ability to write a certain number of words on a given subject in a given time is a prerequisite for any other work. In many freshmen, however, the inability to communicate represents not simply the lack of a skill but a developmental need. The student does have things to say, things important to him that he wants to communicate to others, but *fear* intrudes into the process—fear that he will reveal himself as lacking in grammatical proficiency and thereby invite scorn, or fear that whatever he can say proficiently will be stupid and thereby also an invitation to scorn. Once the problem is recognized as expression and not lack of intelligence, and the teacher's attack moves from skill development to confidence development, these hurdles can fall and skill can be demonstrated. This example suggests no sweeping change in the curriculum or organization of the college. Rather, it points to the need for a college to know its students and their needs better and to approach the art of teaching with greater sophistication and sensitivity.

44

Recognizing that Students Are Different . . .

It is, first of all, important that the college must fully recognize the fact that students are very different. American higher education is only too willing to admit that students have different cognitive abilities, but it must also recognize that students have different interests, different personalities, different emotional needs, and different developmental achievements. It is folly to demand one standardized educational experience for all of them, varying only in major discipline. The school should aim instead to make learning relevant to the rather different strengths and weaknesses, orientations, purposes, and interests of the different student groups. How far a college goes depends on the limits of its imagination, energy, and resources.

Certainly, there is a long way to go before the most elemental principle of developmental psychology can be used by the college in its dealings with students. The length of the distance that must be traveled and the relative obscurity of the route indicates how complete has been our neglect of the personality development of the student. The Committee does not intend to try to specify in detail how the college can serve the diversity of its students, but it believes that developmental education should begin here. Attempts to start elsewhere would be the equivalent of providing frosting with no cake.

. . . And Freshmen Are People

As stated earlier in this report, the freshman year is of critical importance because it is the time when the student's enthusiasm, curiosity, and willingness to work can be snuffed out or reinforced. Part of the problem of the freshman year now is that it confronts the student with academic values that are out of tune with his needs. The university is dedicated to careful, sometimes rather tidily limited, search for evidence and methodically defined conceptualization. The adolescent is much less theoretical than ideological. He likes to work with great, comprehensive ideas, and his ideas are closely related to his own emotions and gropings. He uses ideas both as a guide out of his confusion and as a way to savor what he has not yet experienced. Football player and poet alike are given to discussing the grand topics of religion and sex in their bull sessions.

For a start, the Committee proposes that in the freshman year this ideological bent be given full chance of expression. This may go against the grain of the academic orientation. The inaccuracies, vagueness, and grandiose emotions behind a student's ideas leave most professors aghast. They wish to clamp down almost immediately and give him a sense of what cool, detached, accurate scientific investigation is like, whether in history, literary criticism, or in physics. The student can even conform, because his previous training has already taught him what the coin of the realm is. But this is not what he likes to do, and he gets the sense that his own ideas are unworthy; he feels humiliated and inept. Hence he finds it difficult to connect academic reasoning, and perhaps thought in general, with himself. So we quite naturally produce the anti-intellectuals we complain about.

If we encourage the student's own searches, we can rely on his wanting sooner or later to refine his concepts and test some of his ideas, either by established methods of inquiry or by new ones he might find himself. We should gratefully accept curiosity where we find it, respond as close to the level of the student as we can, and assume that he will not be able to jump several steps at once. We may not have a preconceived plan about where such inquiry will lead, for we need to learn to listen better and follow the student's bent of thinking to sketch out a plan. This will require a rather drastic revision of our standards. Instead of being guided by graduate school manners of performance, as is the rule now, we should have to develop new, individual norms, try to discern the student's purpose, and work with him to realize it. If he prefers philosophy to art, we will both have to understand what he seeks in philosophy and then, if desirable, modify his avoidance of art. We must be alert to the way in which he links ideas to present or anticipated actions or to his past. His ideas ramify over into feelings and actions and we will need to determine where to rely on his own tendencies for growth if left unhindered and where to step in with confrontation or even restraint.

The college must, in short, increase the freshman's opportunities to act independently. (Adults constantly underestimate the intelligence and autonomy of children of all ages, reading a mask of submissiveness as a true face when actually it is put on by young people as a safe way to meet adult arbitrariness and inscrutability. The "mask" also shifts responsibility onto the adults.) The freshman year should end in some feeling of success and competence, something new learnt and some new capacity for enjoyment acquired. When there is little sense of success, the student and his teachers should seek to understand the causes of the failure so that he does not feel overwhelmed or driven into a corner.

46

Such a revamping of the freshman program would play hob with curricula, course work, grade point averages, credits, credit hours, and tuition arrangements, and probably would create great scandal among accrediting organizations. It would, one assumes, be very nice for young people to be able to go through such an experience but there are too many important things to do in the higher educational environment for time to be taken for experimentation. And the time taken for experimentation would delay a student's knuckling down to the task of mastering the subject matter of the various academic disciplines, which so far the college has thought more important.

Students Can Help

The Committee is convinced that the American student is an idealist oriented toward service for his fellow man, but that much of his idealism withers during the college years. It is hard to understand why so few attempts have been made to integrate the desire to serve with the educational experience, for it has long been taken for granted that learning is most effective when it can be directly tied in to some meaningful experience outside the classroom. Nonetheless, the majority of American students never have an opportunity for experiencing the close integration of classroom learning and meaningful service. Apparently, the colleges assume that the students would not be interested. Their failure, for example, to seize the opportunity presented by the volunteer movements of the early 1960s is quite incredible. Colleges and universities did not oppose the volunteer movements, but they made little or no attempt to provide a class which would facilitate the work of the volunteers or help them evaluate their experiences. The classroom, the requirements of course work, and the amassing of credits toward a degree were one thing, and the experiences a student had in his volunteer work were quite something else. He could perhaps be permitted to take time off temporarily from his class work for his volunteer activities, but it occured to few, if any, people that the two kinds of activities logically and naturally ought to be part of one educational experience. And yet college students could participate in many other social tasks, as teachers in schools, as workers with the poor, the handicapped, the sick, and also the prosperous and the successful—wherever there is material for observation and reflection and a chance to serve others. These activities will often confront the student with the seamier side

47

of life, with frustration, injustice, depression. Properly used, such experience cannot only enlarge his sympathies and knowledge, but also help him face his own proclivities for drifting, corruption, and false compromise.

In this respect the church-affiliated schools seem to be particularly guilty of failure. Both because of the ideological commitments which they profess to maintain and because of their link with a nationwide, or in many instances worldwide, network of service organizations, they might have been expected to be leaders in educational reforms integrating the volunteer movements. Yet many church-affiliated schools were less ready than other schools to realize the educational possibilities in the sudden emergence of the volunteer movements.

Even the most aristocratic liberal arts colleges, with their rationale of training for public service, have not found much room in their curricula for the integration of service and learning. Public service is apparently something that is expected to happen after graduation but has little importance in the training of future public servants.

A Question of Meaning . . .

The question of whether it is possible that American higher education, committed as it generally is to philosophical and religious neutrality, is capable of helping the young student in his search for meaning is too vast for the scope of this report. However, a developmental college would be deeply concerned about whether its students were finding any meaning and purpose in their college experiences. It is not enough for the student to amass course credits toward a degree. If he is to be only a performer in college doing busy work, or in his own terms "Mickey Mouse", his skepticism about the possibility of finding meaning in life will be reinforced because he will discover that even in the university, presumably the intellectual core of modern culture, personal meaning is unimportant and the performance of ritual immensely important.

We have for too long assumed that if the student fulfills the requirements, then he will also fulfill himself; that he will obtain personal satisfaction from writing term papers, passing exams, and simply graduating. We have ignored completely the fact that most of our students quite clearly do not believe that much of anything they learn in college is relevant to their problems outside the classroom, or to the lives they plan to lead after graduation, or to an understanding of the complexities of human existence. From the student's viewpoint, what he must undergo through the four years of college is neither useful nor liberal. It does not teach him how to make a living or how to live, and provides neither knowledge nor insight. Far from meeting the human need for competence and belief that what you have achieved was worthwhile, much of what a student has to do in college really reinforces his feelings of senselessness and alienation. He does what is required and overcomes the obstacles set in front of him, but he refuses to commit himself and his faith to the intrinsic value of what he is required to do. Curiously enough, relatively minor changes in our approach to higher education could produce the opposite result.

. . . And Belonging

A developmental college will also be concerned with the student's need to belong. The multiversities have totally abandoned attempts to meet this need, and while the smaller liberal arts colleges can rejoice that they have not made the mistake of the multiversities, it remains to be seen whether in fact they offer any more respect for individuality and freedom than the multiversities. For the multitudes of students that swarm on a university campus, there can be much loneliness and isolation, and the young person's hunger for deeper involvements is, to a considerable extent, unsatisfied.

The creation of communities which would presumably work together, study together, and play together may be of decisive importance, especially in the multiversity, in overcoming the alienation and frustration which are at the root of much student unrest. At least it ought to be possible to convert residence halls into places where small groups of students, with a handful of faculty members, could create a living, learning community. Within these smaller residence halls—which might still be part of much larger complexes—some classroom instruction could take place, there could be some common meals, and as much seminar discussion as possible. This kind of innovation ought to be relatively simple, but it is not likely to occur until there is a major shift in the values of the university, making the importance of this sort of innovation unquestioned. In the meantime, skyscraper dormitories, which would be appropriate as penal institutions but are hardly appropriate as educational houses, will continue to spring up. With some imagination and only moderate extra expenditures, even these could be made more habitable and conducive to reasonably gracious living and serious discussion and reflection. Cultural and human amenities need not be terribly expensive. The fact that they are not provided in most of the new dormitories constructed is merely another indication of how unimportant the student is.

The Obstacle of Competition

In a developmental institution, competition must be drastically reduced. Although competition plays an important role in our society, it is highly dubious whether a society can sustain for long the amount of competitiveness demanded of our young people and remain healthy. The raising of academic standards has become an obstacle to the fulfillment of the very ambitions for excellence that it arouses. It confronts the student with a more rigorous and prolonged series of tests and examinations, stretching from high school into college, beyond college into graduate school, and even beyond that into the life of postdoctoral fellowships or on-the-job evaluations. Such testing is particularly difficult for the adolescent because he has to prove himself in so many other ways, especially in terms of potency as a man or woman. As Anna Freud has said: "There is certainly one point in college life which is counter absolutely to the needs of the adolescent, and that is examinations; for examinations, which symbolically mean to the adolescent that he has to prove whether he has reached the aim of sexual maturity, give rise to enormous amounts of anxiety; and if they cannot be coped with, they then lead to disasters."

This is how a pamphlet by one of the student activists at Berkeley sizes up the situation:

> Your [the student's] routine is comprised of a systematic psychological and spiritual brutality inflicted by a faculty of "well-meaning and nice" men who have decided that your situation is hopeless when it comes to actually participating in serious learning. As an undergraduate you receive a four-year-long series of sharp staccatos: eight semesters, forty courses, one hundred twenty or more units, fifteen hundred to two thousand impersonal lectures, and over three hundred oversized "discussion" meetings. Approaching what is normally associated with learning—reading, writing, and exams— your situation becomes absurd. Over a period of four years you receive

close to fifty bibliographies, ranging in length from one to eight pages, you are examined on more than one hundred occasions, and you are expected to write forty to seventy-five papers. As you well know, reading means "getting into" hundreds of books, many of which are secondary sources, in a superficial manner. You must cheat to keep up. If you don't cheat you are forced to perform without time to think in depth, and consequently you must hand in papers which are almost as shameful as the ones you've cheated on.

A student ought to have a way of knowing what his skills and weaknesses are, but the grade point average is not the most sensible way, humanly or educationally, and in some schools other ways are being tried. Despite the very important part competition plays in supporting the structure of American society, it nonetheless remains a major obstacle to the real goals of higher education.

Points of Order

Similarly, the present administration of rules and disciplines would be gradually phased out in a developmental college. This is not a proposal for anarchy, which, it has sometimes been alleged, student activists seem to be demanding. Not many students, in fact, want anarchy. Their demand is rather for more realistic regulation, meaning rules based on the real needs and problems of the student population. If students had a part in forming and carrying out a college's rules for order, it would probably produce a more, rather than less, orderly campus life. The student's needs for independence and checks on his impulses are much more likely to be met by voluntary acceptance of a disciplinary code he helped write than by strictly enforced obedience to regulations set up, for all practical purposes, to protect the college from the student.

Educating the Faculty

Finally, in a developmental college instructors, besides being well-informed on one or several subjects, would also be quite sophisticated in the psychology of human development, particularly during the young adult years. Such instructors presumably would thoroughly enjoy working with undergraduates and would take delight in facilitating the development of the cognitive as well as the noncognitive dimensions of human personality. Many young men and women do

51

go into careers in higher education precisely because they want to help other young people to grow. It is only their professional training in graduate school that throws cold water on this expectation and turns them into academic researchers. But it is no exaggeration to say that the majority of undergraduate instructors today have little or no natural or acquired skills to facilitate the development of the adolescent personality and in integrating the cognitive with other dimensions of human growth. Whatever their professional skills and reputations may be, faculty members are simply not very good at teaching students.

The developmental college or university understands that the whole man must be educated. It recognizes the vast diversity among students; seeks to integrate the classroom experience with experiences outside the classroom, particularly in the student community and in service beyond its borders; eliminates many forms of competition, and stresses the student's development of his native talents as well as mastery of certain areas where he is relatively weak. It places importance on the freshman year, when it offers the student adventures with great ideas and helps him pursue his own interests at his own pace, until at the end of this year of speculation and experimentation, he has a much clearer idea of what his educational needs and desires really are. It tries to build some kind of faculty-student-administration community on the campus so that study, work, recreation, and life may be shared, and loneliness and isolation minimized.

Even if respect for the dignity and worth of a young person did not justify such an educational approach, it would still be necessary to really teach any subject. No subject, especially a discipline, can intelligently be mastered unless the other developmental needs of a young person can also be met. The developmental college is a necessity from a purely educational viewpoint, no matter how narrowly education is construed. In the past it may have been possible to say that a college could not be simultaneously developmental and liberal, but today when we know so much more about human development, it seems perfectly obvious that the only truly liberal college must be developmental, and the only truly developmental college must be liberal.

The New Liberalism

The Committee stated earlier that it is asking for something very new in higher education, but something that is very much in keeping with the most traditional notions of liberal education. Extending the concept of "liberal" to include the liberating of the whole personality may be the only way that American higher education can resolve its dilemma of educating everybody but for different roles in society.

The classical liberal theory of education argues that the role of the college is to develop the intellects of young people, while at the same time opening to them the riches of the Western cultural tradition. Indeed it is precisely by putting them through the discipline of learning about the arts and sciences which constitute this tradition that young people are expected to develop their ability for intelligent thought and expression. Knowledge and the critical faculty used in assimilating it are good in themselves, independently of any value they have in earning a living or adjusting to life in a complex society. A man equipped with these powers is the liberal man. The Platonic philosopher-king, the Aristotelian free man, the Newmanian gentleman may not be virtuous or ambitious and may even be a nuisance socially, but he is able to think for himself, and to have accomplished this is a sufficient goal for education.

In the classical theory, some of these free men are also qualified to become scholars and will then proceed to the university, where they will get more specialized training in the methods of research they need to push back the frontiers of knowledge. Once again, though, scholarship is a good in itself, apart from its social or financial utility. Just as the free man is the product of the college, the disinterested savant is the product of the university, and the savant presupposes the free man.

Granted that this theory of the purposes of college and university has only rarely, if ever, been achieved in practice, especially in this country, it has had, nonetheless, a pervasive influence on higher education, particularly in Europe. There, and at least until relatively recently in this country, the classical liberal theory of education was essentially an elitist theory. It assumed that only a segment of society was able to be free or a gentleman. The multitrack educational system in European countries assumed that liberal education had to be limited principally to those whose social class prepared them for the responsibilities of such education. More recently, social class has been replaced by intellectual ability as a criterion for entrance into the elite. While the United States has always been somewhat broadminded about admission into its intellectual aristocracy, our rigorous admissions tests and the increasing difficulty of obtaining entrance into the outstanding universities seem to be pushing American society

53

toward an elitist concept of liberal education and scholarship every bit as narrow as that found in nineteenth century England or twentieth century France.

The United States is trying to combine an elitist, aristocratic notion of higher education with an egalitarian notion. On the one hand, every man has a right to a college education, but on the other, only those who have high test scores have a right to get into the schools where they can expect something more than custodial care. And even in these schools early specialization may well replace broad general culture with narrow technical competencies. There is a danger that our attempt to make higher education possible for everybody and at the same time to turn out a skilled technical elite will lead to a complex multitrack system which will do just about everything but produce educated, cultivated human beings.

It seems wrong to assume that only a minority in society is capable of a first-rate educational experience. How high an I.Q. or entrance examination score is necessary for a person to learn to think critically or to enjoy the riches of the Western cultural tradition? The liberalist may be correct when he says that liberal education is for the free man and the gentleman, but the American democratic instinct replies that every American is a free man and a gentleman. There is something profoundly convincing about this belief, but unfortunately the technology of our higher education, indeed of all education, is still essentially elitist. In some sense, this is justified, for there surely is a level of intelligence below which critical thinking becomes extremely difficult, if not impossible. But there is no evidence available to prove that this level is nearly as high as we have set it. The young person who barely makes the admissions standards, such as these may be, for a junior college may still be capable of enjoying Shakespeare or Beethoven, analyzing a political argument, and expressing his thoughts in an articulate and convincing manner. To confine this young person to feeding cards into an IBM machine, to operating a dryer in a beauty salon, or to four years of custodial care before he becomes an auto mechanic or she a housewife, represents a lack of faith in his potentialities. If thus far we have not been able to educate people with an I.Q. of 90 to read poetry or to visit art galleries, or to evaluate critically the weaknesses of a late movie on television, our current failure does not mean that we cannot do so. To resign ourselves to a multitrack system of higher education where the elite get trained in a specialty and the masses are given little better than counseling or custodial care would be to give up the fight before the war begins.

If we are convinced that every American is capable in some way of a liberal education, and that it is essential for all free citizens to be able to think for themselves and to use their leisure intelligently, then higher education has little choice but to attempt to make the traditional liberal education experience available for all its students. This is a task far more difficult than providing custodial care. A liberal education for Everyman would require highly skilled teaching methods and instructors, sophisticated counseling and remedial training, and a profound awareness of the importance of the developmental approach sketched earlier in this chapter. In fact it would probably require a pedagogy that has not even begun to develop. How, indeed, do you teach the junior college student with an I.Q. of 90 to think abstractly or to enjoy a novel that is not a James Bond mystery? But to say it cannot be done and that there is no point in trying or even beginning the research that would sometime enable us to try, would be as snobbish as Aristotle, who thought that only a handful of men were capable of being free, or nineteenth century English educators, who thought that only gentlemen by birth had a right to a gentlemen's education. The alternative to a liberal education for Everyman is the continuation of a technical high school or the blackboard jungle for four more years. Such an educational system would generate class lines as rigid as in any static, aristocratic society; that these lines were drawn by CEEB scores rather than by birth would not make the separation of classes any more acceptable to a democratic society.

The Dilemma of the University Today

The present dilemma in American higher education comes from the seeming contradiction of two propositions: 1) everyone has a right to a college education, and 2) the bright must be given an opportunity to get ahead because a modern society needs its highly trained elite. The Committee contends, however, that the dilemma is only an apparent one and that the two propositions can be resolved by adding a third: Everyone—or at least far, far more than we previously thought—has the potential for critical thought and intelligent enjoyment of the riches of the Western cultural tradition. If American

55

higher education cannot make as vigorous a commitment to the third proposition as it has to the first two, it is heading rather rapidly toward disaster.

It is therefore the firm conviction of this Committee that American higher education must be simultaneously liberal and developmental. It must assume that most young Americans are capable of the kind of intellectual development that has traditionally been the prerogative of the free man. It must also assume that this cognitive development can only take place when the other dimensions of the human personality are also developed, and that an educational institution which focuses narrowly on intellectual learning will fail in its own limited purpose. It may produce clever and skillful technicians, but these technicians are likely to be quite limited human beings, unimaginative and uncreative even within their own disciplines. From such technicians we cannot expect major scientific progress, much less the kind of insight and wisdom that is necessary to cope with the implications of scientific progress. As American higher education awaits anxiously the inundation of the 1970s, it must realize that it will either tread the path which we have marked liberal-developmental, or will, within a decade or two, develop a higher educational system composed of highly sophisticated technical schools, on the one hand, and extended blackboard jungles, on the other. Such a prospect is not a happy one to contemplate.

V

Recommendations

THIS REPORT WAS written to bring attention to the possibility of developmental higher education and to suggest the style and method with which colleges ought to attempt the possible. Chapter IV outlined broad areas where colleges might begin experimentation. This chapter contains some more specific recommendations, but it is not intended as a how-to-do-it blueprint. The vast diversity of American higher education would make a blueprint impossible, even if it were desirable. In different schools there will be different points at which to begin, different pressures for reform, and different resources that can be utilized. This Committee's recommendations can therefore claim only to be illustrative and not programmatic.

These recommendations call for a major qualitative change in planning for the future of higher education. The Committee has no quarrel with the computer experts, the technical planners, and the budgetary wizards who are telling us how many students, teachers, and classrooms we will need by 1980 and how much money the projected expansion will cost. The quantitative specialists are competent in their field, and their work is indispensable to the survival and growth of our colleges, but it is not enough, for they are not concerned with the character of education. It takes another kind of planner to consider and envision the quality of human relationships in the college environment. And the improvement of this quality is as

57

desirable and probably more necessary than improvement of the physical plant. The alternative to the dream of developmental education envisaged by this Committee is a nightmare.

In this respect the university is no different than the rest of American society, which must face as its most critical problem the question of whether affluence will make possible a richer and fuller human existence or depersonalize human relationships in a great nightmare of mechanized, computerized, standardized living. Industrialism seems to bear within itself a strong strain toward impersonal bigness, even though ample research demonstrates that after a certain point sheer size becomes inefficient and dysfunctional precisely because it dehumanizes. It is not yet clear whether there exists in our republic sufficient will to recreate within the gigantic structures of industrial society smaller substructures and communities where the human spirit can develop its potential as has never been possible before in the history of the human race. Big business, big labor, big government, big military, and big universities must be decentralized if they are to stay alive, for mechanization will, in the long run, destroy the very sources of vitality and creativity on which all human institutions depend for their survival.

The quality of relationships in higher education therefore must be improved not simply because it will enable students to spend happy and more fulfilling years in college or because many of the present conditions in higher education are intolerable, but primarily because unless trends toward giantism and dehumanization are reversed, the college will not be able to educate even the technician. The argument for developmental education is, in the last analysis, that even technicians cannot be trained unless it is recognized that they are something more than functionaries—that they are also human beings, and as such they can perform effectively only when their basic emotional needs are fulfilled. Everyone wants a face, not a mask.

For these reasons, the Committee's recommendations call for an improvement in the quality of human relationships in the college, an improvement which will require far better integration of the cognitive and noncognitive dimensions of human growth.*

*Although the primary concern of this report is the student in higher education, it should be noted that unless the quality of relationships for faculty and administrators is also improved, no lasting effect can be had on the life of the student. Colleges and universities must become more human environments for everyone involved, or they will become so for no one.

58

Experimentation and Research

1. There must be a proliferation of experimentation and experimenting colleges. Every major American multiversity ought to engage in wide experimentation in modifications of the teacher-pupil encounter and the living conditions on its campus. The best experimental colleges would attempt to use all the knowledge currently available about teaching, learning, and adolescent development, and their efforts would aim to combine living, learning, working, social service, and recreation into one integrated educational experience in which small groups of students and faculty would participate together, regardless of the rigid demands of course work, credits, and degrees. The university should say to a handful of its more gifted faculty and administrators, "Find some students who are interested in the experiment you want to try and then go ahead and do it. We will guarantee to do all in our power to get the students into graduate schools, and we will keep the accrediting agencies at bay. Go ahead and experiment to your heart's content and don't worry about the lamentations of administrators and the wailing of faculty colleagues. You may have to work outside the structure of the guild-dominated regular course of instruction, but don't worry about the guilds. We'll protect you from them too."

While it can be expected that some multiversities will take the lead in experimenting in developmental education, it may very well be that the leadership will come from other segments of American higher education—from the state, community, junior, and small liberal arts colleges, and some of the religiously-affiliated colleges. Since they are smaller and less dependent on federal research dollars, many of these institutions ought to have a greater degree of flexibility for experimentation. Furthermore, since their faculties, for weal or for woe, have not made it into the academic big time, they are under somewhat less constraint to live up to the demands of the guilds. Unfortunately, these "lesser" institutions, which educate some 80 percent of American students, serve almost in bondage the demands of the multiversities. Asking these institutions to take the lead in experimentation is demanding a great deal, proposing a revolution in fact, but for many of these institutions it is the sort of revolution that may be imperative for survival. They will only exist if they can offer their clientele something unique which the great state universities cannot match. While the state colleges and junior colleges need not be concerned about survival, they should surely realize that they will only achieve academic respectability through innovation.

There would be some risks run, of course, in such experimental colleges, but it is difficult to imagine that they could do a worse job of coping with the cognitive and other needs of young people than our present colleges. Structural reform probably will not come from within the present system. The spin-off school which is in some vague way affiliated with the multiversity and still enjoys the freedom to experiment is the most efficient way of bringing innovation, progress, and reform to American higher education.

2. Much more intensive research should be undertaken on the educational applications of developmental psychology and also on the means of providing a liberal education for those who score relatively low on the I.Q. scale. This research would be greatly facilitated by combining several different experimental colleges on one campus.

It is incredible that American colleges spend so much money on recruiting and admitting students and so little on attempts to measure the impact of college on the development of the students' personalities. It is also astonishing that the work done by clinical researchers has not been tested on a wider scale. The themes of alienation, apathy, and privatism have been discussed in the literature but have not been tested on large and representative samples of students. One of the premises on which this report is based—that the college years see the conversion of idealism into cynicism—is strongly supported by impressionistic evidence but has not been documented by research. The extraordinarily useful ideas of Erik Erikson on identity and ideology have not been used to discover how the young adult develops his self-concept and world view, save with very small samples of students. Nor do we know what impact different styles of instruction, different organization of curricula, different institutional structures have either on the learning experience or on personality development. We are not even sure that the college makes much difference at all, though the members of the Committee do not believe that the personality is so determined by earlier experiences that college *cannot* play an important role. The possibilities for useful research are almost unlimited—once we admit that learning and personality development are inseparable.

RECOMMENDATIONS

Organization of Instruction

1. The whole freshman year should be viewed as an orientation to learning rather than the first year of academic instruction. Freshman orientation should not be one week of adjustment to a college, but a whole year of acculturation to an entirely new and exciting activity—serious and systematic thought—and a year of integrating the pursuit of skill and knowledge with the search for identity and intimacy.

2. No matter how much it may confuse schedules or course loads and no matter how many new faculty personnel must be hired, colleges should strive to have as many individual tutorials or seminars and as few lecture-hall, particularly large lecture-hall, classes as possible. The kinds of information usually presented in the lecture hall could probably be presented even more efficiently and effectively through the new teaching machines. There is little or no reason to have a person appear in front of 500 students, but much reason to have him appear around a table of seven, eight, or ten or even fifteen students.

3. Competition in all colleges should be reduced. Grades should be optional, and the student should be permitted to settle for a pass-fail alternative if he so desires. Undergraduate institutions may have to defy the graduate schools to accomplish this reform, but they should ask the graduate school faculty how good a predictor of performance and productivity in later life undergraduate grades really are.

Faculty

1. A new kind of faculty must appear, composed of men and women whose primary concern is the facilitation of the learning experiences of students and helping them derive personal meaning from these experiences. These faculty members will be competent in one or several academic disciplines, but their commitment will turn from the kind of professional research they can report in the academic journals to the developmental experience of undergraduates. Given the expected surplus of Ph.D.'s in the early 1970s, it should be relatively easy to find trained personnel who would be interested in such work. Indeed a good number of the current personalist generation of undergraduate and graduate students would undoubtedly find

far more life satisfactions in this sort of work than in being academic researchers. The new faculty must be required to understand in practice the basic principles of human psychological development, and they must be committed to aiding the emotional development of their students. Their status in the university must be at least equal to that of faculty who are interested primarily in research, and this equal status must be reinforced by the only means that is effective in American society—equal, if not superior, pay.

In addition, it would be extraordinarily helpful if some teachers were not from the academic community. No disrespect for the worldliness or sophistication of the college professor is meant by this recommendation, but students would benefit greatly from occasional and even frequent contact with instructors whose primary orientation is not academic. The world is made up of vast varieties of people, and despite the increase in the number of professional academicians, they are still but a small minority of the human race. For the college to facilitate the fullest growth of the human personality, it ought to reflect the world beyond the campus in every feasible way. Besides, the nonacademic sector of society might be greatly enriched if some of their members had more frequent contact with college students and faculty.

2. The power of the professional academic guilds over undergraduate instruction must be broken. Faculty veto groups, however powerful, can no longer be permitted to block reform in undergraduate education, to specify what educational experiences a young person must have before he is admitted to graduate school, and to ignore the developmental dimension of higher education. It is to be expected that a vast number, perhaps the overwhelming majority, of faculty members will agree as individuals with the basic contentions of this report. However, when they are called upon to act as members of their professional guilds, they often find serious conflict between their personal beliefs about the nature of education and the kind of stand they feel they must take to preserve their union. It would be idle to expect that the power of the faculty over undergraduate instruction can easily be reduced, even though the way this power is currently exercised has little or nothing to do with the education of young people.

It may well be necessary to completely divorce undergraduate training from graduate training, both in the universities and the colleges, since undergraduate schools are too frequently viewed by all faculty as stepping stones to graduate schools. The goals of undergraduate education and graduate education are both quite valid, but they are not the same. It is difficult to see how undergraduate education can succeed, particularly in integrating cognitive and non-cognitive learning, if it is not able to operate independently of the demands of the graduate departments.

The World Inside

1. The Committee urges increased student participation in educational policymaking. Not that students are wiser than the faculty or administrators, but they do have insight into the meaning of their educational experiences which ought to be important in making policy and administrative decisions. Student representation at the very highest governing levels of the college—even on the board of trustees, if possible—is also necessary to prevent in the future a repetition of student victimization by the professional guilds and college administrators.

2. The Committee strongly recommends wide democratization of rulemaking and enforcing on the college campus. This democratization is undoubtedly going to take place in any event, and administrators would be well-advised to do it with good grace rather than as a result of ever more insistent student pressure. On this point, as well as in our other recommendations, we are again insisting that the improvement of the quality of human relationships and efficient education are inseparable.

3. We recommend that the college take a hard look at its housing and eating facilities, and ask whether they promote or retard the formation of human community and a style of life that is conducive to the development of respect for the good and the beautiful. Unless physical structures of the university are drastically reformed, it will be quite impossible for the kinds of student communities which will facilitate rather than impede the serious work of higher education to emerge on the college campus.

The task of creating an environment conducive to human growth is not an easy one even on the college campus, but it is far more difficult when the student is a commuter, as are more than half of American college students. The problem of integrating cognitive and noncognitive development in a commuter college is staggering, and at first glance seems to be almost insoluble. The commuter's contact with his school can be quite transient: a few hours each day in the classroom, and then quickly off to his job or his home and family. The colleges's opportunity to integrate the "out-of-classroom" experience with the classroom experience in these circumstances seems to be quite minimal. Indeed, the basic friendship groups in the student's life may be composed of people who do not attend the same college or any college. Most, if not all, of his noncognitive development occurs beyond the influence of the college, and his college experience may be completely segmented from the rest of his life.

We surely do not propose to offer any answers to this problem, especially since research and even theory on the subject is so scarce. But if the assumptions upon which this report is based have any validity at all, it follows that the commuter colleges must be concerned with the noncognitive development of their students as any other college must, and that they face an even greater challenge to find the methods and structures that will enable them to act on this concern.

4. We further urge colleges and universities to recognize that all their administrative personnel play a role in education, since they are the ones the students most frequently deal with. One wonders how much of the student unrest could be attributed to authoritarian police, rude clerks, hostile and unfriendly secretaries, and testy tellers. If the institution as a whole is devoted to promoting the full human development of its students, then all of its personnel should be trained to understand the needs of this development. No matter how unimportant a staff position may seem to the administration and faculty, it must be recognized that the students have to deal with many of these people constantly.

The World Outside

1. We think it particularly important that before the volunteer era ends in complete disillusionment, colleges and universities give serious consideration to how volunteer service can be closely integrated with the educational experience. We disagree with those who hold that volunteer service should become expected or obligatory. But we do think that American colleges should stress that a period

of volunteer service, far from being extraordinary or unusual, is perfectly normal and that they are only too happy to cooperate with, rather than tolerate, this service. We contend that this attitude toward voluntarism ought to be maintained not only because voluntarism is a good thing in itself, but because it presents an excellent educational opportunity.

2. There should be more flexible arrangements for spending the required time in college. Even though 60 per cent of American students do not graduate from the college in which they enrolled after leaving high school, colleges have shown little willingness to give and make students feel free to take time off to work for brief periods or to engage in service, either in this country or abroad.

The tyranny of prerequisites and sequence of courses is such that he who departs from the straight and narrow path to graduation is expected to pay severe penalties for his idiosyncratic behavior. In our judgment, not only should these penalties be eliminated, but to some extent, it might be very healthy if colleges actually encouraged personal experimentation by their students. The time they take off is more than likely to contribute to their development and increase their interest in professional training.

Conclusion

The Committee is under no illusion that any or all of its recommendations will provide the answer to the boredom, frustration, apathy, bitterness, and alienation which many observers find characteristic of college students today. The roots of these problems are in our culture, and educational reform cannot by itself change a whole culture. But our recommendations provide material for beginning an educational reform that would open to the student the possibility of improving our society and its culture. A good education ought not to be expected to provide all the answers, but at least it can offer the raw material for vision and hope.

We are therefore interested primarily in improving the quality of American higher education. We are convinced that the knowledge of human development from the behavioral sciences now makes possible a wider vision of what the school can accomplish and of more effective ways of teaching. American higher education has not paid enough attention to human development as a part of its mission, and

65

the time has come for this neglect to end—*in the name of better education.*

In insisting that higher education must take into account the developmental needs of students, we do not deny that the liberal developmental college we have described would be a far more pleasant, comfortable, and humane place in which to live. We are in sympathy with as much humanity and comfort as can possibly be offered to anybody in the world. But the educational reforms we are insisting upon are not luxuries.

American society is curiously ambivalent about its young. It showers riches and benefits upon them and then simultaneously demands that they be tough, hard, and aggressive. It pampers them but insists the young people ought not to be pampered. The suggestions we have made have nothing to do with pampering or with softening or hardening. They have everything to do with the essential prerequisites of education; that these prerequisites make life more enjoyable is all to the good. But because they will make the student's life more enjoyable does not mean that they are, for that reason, any the less necessary.